SHOES OF PEACE

on the

DESERT ROAD

Sarah Ivette Morales

ISBN 979-8-89130-583-0 (paperback)
ISBN 979-8-89130-584-7 (digital)

Christian Faith Publishing
832 Park Avenue
Meadville, PA 16335
www.christianfaithpublishing.com

Printed in the United States of America

*To my beautiful loving family, especially Mom,
Joe, Dad, Andrea, Mr. and Mrs. Morales
Thank you for all the prayers and love*

*My inspirational best friends—Andrea, Maria, Rebekah, and Vanesa
I'm forever grateful for your friendship*

*To every wonderful staff member at MD Anderson, you give
patients hope and comfort in the most difficult circumstances
Thank you for your dedication every day*

*To my reasons for fighting every day—Randy,
Melanie, and Natalie—I love you forever*

Introduction

I wrote this out of love for my two little girls. There were times when I didn't think I would make it, but I kept going for my family. I felt compelled to share my story to help those who need hope and further the promise I made to God. I am a patient for life, but I will continue to live because of God's great mercy. I leaned on scripture, devotionals, and the power of music.

I was told many times I looked good. I would tell them, "It's not something you can see on the outside; it's internal."

We can think of ourselves in our spiritual walk. We may seem fine, but on the inside, we are broken. The walk is not an easy one, but walking with God is far better than being without him. God is the reason I am here today.

To all who deal with any type of cancer, illness, loss, or depression, walking in faith is no easy task. Jesus himself had to walk alone and knew what ultimately had to be done to save us.

Keep fighting, allow yourself to feel those emotions, but don't stay down in the pit. Pray and surrender all to him; these burdens are far too heavy for us to carry. God gives us strength to endure if you allow him in your heart. I've been down in the valley and high on that mountain. It comes down to five things for me: God, faith, family, friends, and a positive attitude. My hope is you find peace, comfort, and joy. May God bless you!

My precious loves, there will be trials and tribulations in this life that will seem unfair, unbearable, and unimaginable. I know this to be true, the unimaginable happened in my life. Diagnosed with inflammatory breast cancer at thirty-eight had me feeling a plethora of emotions, mostly sadness. But what do you do during the dark seasons of life? Pray! My hope is that you continue to seek God in all things and walk in peace each day of your lives. God is always good, girls!

I love you always,
Mom

In the Eye of the Storm

I learned of my cancer over the phone; my nerves were ready to electrify my body from anxiously waiting. The kind nurse apologized for not being able to deliver the information sooner. My right breast is negative, but my left breast has two spots in the two o'clock and five o'clock areas. My heart sank and I thought, *how?*

At the time, my parents were over at our house visiting. They said, "You are strong, and you can get through this." I felt like, what does strong have anything to do with cancer? No family history, perfectly healthy body, and I exercise three to four days a week. Just six months ago, I was even eating better in order to prepare for my sister's wedding. Those bridesmaids' dresses can be brutal! Cancer was the last thing I would have ever imagined, but here I am.

My precious loves, sometimes in life, we are blindsided. When I learned of my diagnosis, I knew this was beyond what I could bear. Only God knows the plans in our lives and although things may feel like a punishment, it is not. God is always good, and he loves us. When you were little, we used to sing "He's Got the Whole World in His Hands" and "Jesus Loves Me." There is a verse that says, "Little ones belong to him, they are weak, but he is strong." Remember to hold on in your faith; life is better with God by your side.

The LORD gives perfect peace to those whose
faith is firm. (Isaiah 26:3 CEV)

Doctor's Appointment

On December 23, 2022, I attended my appointment for further explanation of my cancer diagnosis. I sat there with your father and my dear friends, Rebekah and Vanesa. Rebekah was very well-versed in cancer terminology because, sadly, both her parents dealt with cancer. I listened intently trying to take in all the details of my diagnosis of stage 3 invasive carcinoma. The oncologist addresses my regimen and is confident she can handle my case. I immediately say I want treatment right away, but I am also trying to seek treatment at MD Anderson. She tells me that she is not offended if patients go and goes on to state that it would be a Christmas miracle if I get in. The comment only set a spark in me to prove her wrong, and I considered it a challenge.

Leaving that office, I learned about having a mastectomy and the long road ahead. On the way home, Rebekah just looked at me in the back seat and said, "You are incredibly brave." I told her that I have to be and that I don't have a choice for my family, husband, and the girls. Rebekah's mother was a true fighter all the way to the end. She was a model of how to not let cancer break one's spirit. I just prayed to God, "Please bring peace in my heart and strength to endure."

Interestingly enough, we had a Christmas party planned that night, and we enjoyed yourselves. Honestly, sometimes, I find myself thinking that I don't have cancer and then *bam,* back to reality.

Cancer can sometimes show no obvious signs, and so many go about their day without even knowing they have it. I am just so thankful that I have a support system to help me get through this.

My precious loves, this was one of the hardest days to get through. I couldn't have done it without peace in my heart that only God can provide. Melanie and I would pray a little prayer thanking Jesus for everything, including protecting her through the night. My hope is that prayer would remain a constant in your life. Sometimes we get so sidetracked in the business of life. Your father and I have always been hard workers, but don't let work distract you from what is truly important to sustain you, and that is God.

> Don't worry about anything, but pray about everything. With thankful hearts offer up your prayers and requests to God. (Philippians 4:6 CEV)

MD Anderson

After learning my results, I called the new patient hotline thanks to Rebekah, who made me enroll through the website. Explaining my diagnosis again, I just began to feel disbelief. Why am I doing this? No family history; I feel fine; and it is cancer! The operator explains how he is connecting me with the right people and that I should be receiving a call right away. I received a call the following morning and completed the rest of the process. Thank goodness it was covered by your father's insurance. I also began to feel a bit angry about the whole medical process because worrying about coverage should not be an issue. Your father and I got final appointment dates, and we planned to take off after my appointment with another specialist.

Long drive, but we try to make the best of it by talking and listening to music. I see the pain in his eyes, and it's like he can't believe this is happening. We hold each other's hands and continue to have faith. We make it to MD Anderson and begin a series of six tests in a span of two days. MRIs, I wish upon no one! I'm not severely claustrophobic, but the worst one was the brain MRI. The test ran for forty-five minutes, and the banging noise was like an annoying car alarm. I breathe in, asking the Lord for strength and retracing my thoughts to my family and my beautiful girls. I even humanized the machine by thinking that it is only trying to figure out what else is going on in my body. I didn't name it—I couldn't focus on that—rather, I only focused on this test being completed to move forward with the treatment plan. I had to remind myself of being brave and being the example for you girls.

My precious loves, I hope you never have to endure cancer. Family has always been important for your father and I. Throughout this process, my Tia Ofelia would send me encouraging messages daily. I thought this one in particular would be good for you to read:

Have Faith…
God is always with you, though it may not seem so. Have Hope…
God's love surrounds you much more than you know. Have Peace…
God has a special plan for you. Have Joy…
For always, come what may, God will help to see you through.

Game Plan

I met Dr. Valero and learned about my diagnosis of inflammatory breast cancer, a rare cancer form that affects 10 percent of people my age. I'm thirty-eight. I listen intently, trying to ignore my heart sinking down to my stomach. He explains like a college professor with visuals that he was drawing on patient paper. I appreciate the lesson because all the medical jargon is like another language. He explains the need to have a PET scan done to check for cancer in other parts of the body.

Later that day, I continued to my next and last appointment—the PET scan. I took that scan like a champ because it was only fifteen minutes. Mind you, I always close my eyes during the tests. I remember my friend Vanesa's words, "The mind is a powerful thing and it affects the rest of your body, so think positive and stay strong."

My sweet girls, I can't even begin to explain the feelings I experienced. However, I do know that the only reason I was able to hear it without breaking down was because of God's peace. I would read devotionals and scriptures; the following words helped me. I hope they help you one day if you ever feel in complete despair.

Devotional reading ("New Year, New Mercies: A 15-Day Devotional with Paul Tripp" from the YouVersion app):

> "You need to remind yourself again and
> again of His wise and loving control, not because
> that will immediately make your life make sense,
> but because it will give you rest and peace in

those moments that all of us face at one time
or another -when life doesn't seem to make any
sense."

With all your heart you must trust the LORD
and not your own judgment. Always let him lead
you, and he will clear the road for you to follow.
(Proverbs 3:5–6 CEV)

Moving Onward

On the way home from Houston, we had to stop somewhere so I could do a Zoom call with my doctor. I learned more about my diagnosis—spots were found in my lungs and spine. Therefore, I was considered stage 4. These words were so hard to hear, but I knew in my heart I had to keep thinking positive for my family and you precious girls. I wanted to see you grow old and to see what you would become. Those thoughts of "what if" would creep up. I cried so much and just let the tears flow. What could I have done differently to change this? Did I miss the warning signs? I've never felt so defeated.

Your father assured me that there was nothing that I did to cause this cancer. He reminded me to keep thinking positive and if anyone can get through this, it's me. He said, "You are strong." But what is the definition of strong? Enduring pain when you can't see the end? I just let my tears out and made the choice. I needed to keep a positive attitude because God has come through for me in many tough times: motherhood, career, the transition to stay-at-home mom. Later that day, we made it home to see you, our babies. You were happy to see us, and we were happy to be home.

My sweet loves, you need to allow yourselves to feel. Jesus himself wept, and this shows us that he understands our human emotions.

> When Jesus saw that Mary and the people with her were crying, he was terribly upset and asked, "Where have you put his body?" They

replied, "LORD, come and you will see." Jesus started crying, and the people said, "See how much he loved Lazarus." (John 11: 33–36 CEV)

Chemotherapy

Preparing for chemotherapy gave me a sense of urgency to exercise in preparation for battle. I only knew of the fragile state that is associated with cancer. However, that is not the case. Chemo affects everyone so differently, and my only hope was to avoid vomiting and nausea—it sounded awful. I had smooth pregnancies and didn't experience all the typical symptoms. I prayed and just said, "Lord, give me the strength to endure."

We make it to the Sugarland location, which helps to avoid all the city-highway traffic of Houston. As we make our way in, I just remind myself, *You have cancer, and this is the way to beat it. You have to endure it, no matter what comes.*

Cancer is a mind game that comes in waves. One minute I'm doing fine, enjoying time with family and my girls, then I'll just stop and realize that I've got cancer. How did it come to this? If you had told me five years ago that I would be in this fight, I would've said, *how?* No family history, no real sickness, good overall health, but cancer still came?

Every day, you hear stuff about people dying and then you say, "Oh what a shame, how sad." I didn't want to be that story, so I continue to fight and keep my head high. When I'm home, I get teary-eyed listening to Disney songs with my girls. I try to take it all in—*I'm still here!* Pastor Polo once told me that someone out there needs to hear my testimony. I pray that one day I will share my story, and it will help others go through this journey.

My precious loves, during this time, I had to do a lot of prep-talking to myself. I was experiencing tremendous fear about chemotherapy and cancer overall. I prayed for strength and peace that only God can provide during this process. My hope is that you remember to allow God to strengthen you during those times of doubt and fear.

Let the spirit renew your thoughts and attitudes. (Ephesians 4:23 NLT)

Staying at Home

Back to the routine. I have to keep up with my girls and ensure there is normalcy. Thankfully, I'm in good spirits and feeling good after chemotherapy. There were minor aches, but no need for medication. I'm keeping positive and thankful to be home—no tests, no clinic. Your father has been my rock. The other night, we just hugged each other for a long time. We didn't need words because we could just feel each other's emotions of some relief, tiredness, and the acceptance of the long road to recovery. He looked at me and said I was going to be just fine.

My loves, I hope you have a wonderful and supportive husband. There are times in this life when words are not needed; you just need to be there to support the person you love. God loves us, and his love will never fail us. Remember this!

Your love is faithful, LORD, and even the clouds in the sky can depend on you. Your decisions are always fair. They are firm like mountains, deep like the sea, and all people and animals are under your care. Your love is a treasure, and everyone finds shelter in the shadow of your wings. (Psalms 36:5–7 CEV)

Wigs and More

My acceptance of losing my hair was actually easier than I thought. Crazy that a wig would be something like an experiment for me. I haven't been styling my hair or coloring it since even before COVID-19. My haircuts have involved DIY projects with hair clippers. Your father ordered a hair cap, and I tried it on. We both laughed a bit. I joked that eventually I'm going to be a hairless piglet, which is the pet name your father has for me.

Rebekah sent me a link that night to check out wigs. I just looked at the styles and tried to imagine myself with a wig. My sister's wedding is coming up. Part of me is so thankful that I'll be able to attend, now that I know how my body responds to chemo.

The following morning, my parents visited after returning from their cruise. Even before my diagnosis, I told them to please go and continue their cruises because normalcy is what I needed to help me. They earned their retired life, and I'm glad they could continue their adventures because it is good to be in decent health for traveling.

During their visit, I got a call from MD Anderson about the IBC group. I asked, "I'm so sorry, what does that stand for again?"

The woman states, "Inflammatory Breast Cancer group, to aid in research as to why this happens in young women like yourself."

My thoughts were like, *Oh my gosh, others like me…young and living life and then suddenly all that changed with a cancer diagnosis.* I stated, "Oh yes, of course I would because research saves."

I pray that my girls will not have to endure cancer of any kind. Still, continued research aids in future treatments that will help save lives. I stand with others in the fight, and I hope to meet others in my position one day.

My precious loves, we have to understand that God is so wonderful that he gives us the freedom of choice. I could've looked at my situation with an attitude of grimness and despair. However, I held on to God's word. Satan will do his best to bring us down, so we must cast out those negative thoughts that are not from God.

> When I was really hurting, I prayed to the LORD. He answered my prayer, and took my worries away. The LORD is on my side, and I am not afraid of what others can do to me. (Psalms 118:5–6 CEV)

Chemo Aftermath

I thought I would be in the clear without any real symptoms of chemo. However, last night, I experienced the most aching back pain. No matter how I lay down, I just felt it radiating on my spine. I finally gave in and told your father that I needed the pain medication I was prescribed. I didn't feel relief until an hour in and I finally passed out on the guest bed. I slept like a rock because the previous night, I had a little insomnia. I tell myself it's only a couple more times of this and then on to the next step.

However, I began to feel defeated. How am I going to get through this and for how long? It's normal to just want to move on with things, but I have to be patient and let chemo do what it needs to do. I wish I knew someone like me, young and experiencing this. Hopefully, soon I will be able to join a support group. Until then, I'll put on a brave face for my family. I hope one day I can look back and say, "God, you helped me at my worst," and share my testimony.

My sweet girls, I consider myself a strong person, but this disease can definitely take a toll physically and mentally. Music is so powerful, especially worship music. I'm sure that both of you have a love for music; that comes from me and Grandpa Rodriguez. I listened to a variety of songs to help me remember God's strength. A word or a verse would speak to my soul and it felt incredibly healing.

My power and my strength come from the
LORD, and he has saved me. (Psalms 118:14 CEV)

Family

Thankful that I have such a huge support system. How can we face this alone? I feel for those who don't have family nearby. As Hispanics, we tend to be very close. Family is our everything. Blessings are indeed not only for family but also great friends who ask how I am doing or call just to see how things are going with treatment.

Day by day, I just think, *Sarah, you are alive!* If the Lord were done with me on earth, I would already be gone. Unfinished business is all I can think of. I hope one day to inspire my precious daughters and others who feel lost due to this disease. Family is everything, that's all I can say.

My loves, there will be times when you just want to give up. This is normal because we are not meant to carry these burdens on our own. We must surrender our way of thinking and handling of our situations. Faith in the Lord has been an example for me; I remember going to church with my mother and faithfully devoted grandmothers. Life is complicated, but God can give you the clarity you need.

> We never give up. Our bodies are gradually dying, but we ourselves are being made stronger each day. These little troubles are getting us ready for an eternal glory that will make all our troubles seem like nothing. Things that are seen don't last forever, but things that are not seen are eternal. This is why we keep our minds on the things that cannot be seen. (2 Corinthians 4:16–18 CEV)

MD Anderson

As I come back to this place, I think of new possibilities and have a new hope. Strange that I would feel this way. As I see others around me, I just think, *Darn, we are all in this fight.* I joke with the nurse that living older is a blessing and a goal. People are taken too soon, and it seems easy to question God. However, we can't question God; we will never understand his ways. I hope my daughters understand this, and I pray that they have the same attitude when tough times come ahead. Where would I be without my faith in God? I can't imagine because I know I wouldn't have peace.

My loves, don't let your circumstances steal your joy. If you read the Bible, you'll understand that many followers struggled but were saved by the Lord's grace and mercy. Things may not always end up to our liking, but God knows what we need and what he is protecting us from. I've had some bad experiences, and by God's grace, things worked out in the end for the better. Pray for peace in your heart in times of trouble.

> Cast all your anxiety on him because he cares for you. (1 Peter 5:7 NIV)

> Come to me, all you who are weary and burdened, and I will give you rest. (Matthew 11:28 NIV)

All in the Fight

Today was my last appointment, and it is for a spine biopsy. The procedure wasn't as bad as I imagined. I prayed for peace, and I could hear my heartbeat on the monitor machine. The machine is not as intimidating, and I didn't feel claustrophobic. I even took a little nap thanks to those meds that relaxed me. When I was done, we exited Mays Clinic and I sat out on the benches, waiting for our shuttle. I look to my left and see this man that reminded me of Terry Bradshaw. Lo and behold, it was him! I decided to get my phone and took a picture of him talking to a couple. I had no idea he was in the fight too. Wow, sometimes we don't realize that no matter the status, it can happen to anyone.

I showed your father the picture and he was like, "Oh man, that's him!" I sent the picture to my father and he said, "Yes, he has cancer and kept it private." I understand, but I feel like we should share the testimony because it helps others in the fight and gives them hope. We need it now more than ever.

My sweet girls, sometimes it feels like we are alone, but you must remember you are not. There are others who may feel like you and are fighting the same battles. No one is immune from the pain and suffering of this world. God's grace and love will help you through, girls, just seek him. I would like you to read this devotional that helped me. This is from *Hope When It Hurts: Biblical Reflections to Help You Grasp God's Purpose in Your Suffering* by Kristen Wetherell and Sarah Walton:

"Friend, this life is filled with circumstances
that will leave us questioning or even denying

God's goodness if we live by what we see, rather than by faith in what God has promised. The choice we face is a daily one. We can choose to either trust what we see and define what's good for us ourselves, and grow annoyed with God and doubt his goodness, or we can live by faith in a crucified Savior and let him define what's good for us, even if it means exercising our faith muscles as we choose to trust him over what we can see and feel.

So let's come to Christ with our doubts and weaknesses and ask him to give us the faith to take our eyes away from what we can see in front of us and lift our eyes again to the cross-because that is where we will find assurance and confidence in the undeserving goodness and faithfulness of our heavenly Father. Is God good? Yes. He died for you."

It Is Just Hair

Part of me thought just maybe I would be one of those rare ones who don't lose their hair. The fallout began while we were staying in the hotel. I started seeing more hair in the shower than usual. The following day we did my appointment with MD Anderson, and all went okay. While at home, I had my hair down in a headband and while doing chores around the house, I noticed that my hair began knotting and gathered at the bottom in a horrible knot. I have no choice but to take it out and see the clump. Part of me thinks, *Okay, chemo is doing its job.* However, the other part of me is sad. My girls have no idea what I'm going through. It's good because you are still little, but it's also sad because if you were older, you would be my biggest cheerleaders. I can't just show up bald—you won't understand, and it would be so confusing. How would a three-year-old and one-year-old process me without hair?

My wig has already been ordered, and I immediately try it on. I need to start getting myself adjusted to wigs. I'm going to stay positive and experiment with styles. I just need to get adjusted to my first look…no hair!

My precious loves, sometimes we have to look at the bigger picture. I lost a big part of being a woman, and it hurt to look in the mirror. However, I knew that it was only for a little while and that I was alive, for which I was beyond grateful. I was more afraid of scaring you girls, and it didn't take long to come clean with my bald head. You girls just looked at me, touched my head, and moved on.

> You have turned my sorrow into joyful dancing. No longer am I sad and wearing sackcloth. I thank you from my heart, and I will never stop singing your praises, my LORD and my God. (Psalms 30:11–12 CEV)

Parental Support

My parents made the trip with me to MD Anderson. It felt like I was a kid again, even before marriage and kids. I even managed to do a little shopping, and it felt nice.

MD Anderson was a strange feeling probably for my parents. They were shocked to see people from all nationalities, mostly senior citizens. I think it helps them realize how in great shape they are and how blessed they are to not have to deal with this type of disease. For me, it was strange because you have people in their fifties and above with their children helping them. In my case, it was me getting help from my parents. I just remind myself that I got this and that I can do this.

My sweet girls, you have no idea how much all your grandparents helped us through this process. We were able to have more peace of mind knowing you were in good hands. If you become parents, you will understand how difficult it can be to leave your children in someone else's care. Someone once told me that grandparents are the second-best thing when it comes to taking care of your children, and I couldn't agree more!

Port Placement

Five in the morning was wake-up time for surgery to report at 6 a.m. to MD Anderson. I wake up and just pray for the Lord to give me strength and help us all get through this. I don't feel nervous until I'm sitting alone with just my mom in the waiting area. I remind myself that I can do this and to look at how far I've come since my diagnosis.

I completed the first round of chemo and all the series of tests. My name is called, and I change into a hospital gown before settling in the bed. I just tell myself, *Okay here we go*, in my head. The nurse checks my vitals and begins to chat about driving in Houston, and I laugh. One thing I've told myself is to not let this rob my spirit and joy. Laughter is the best medicine, and even science has backed that up. More nurses show up, and we make small talk about our babies. She was pregnant with her third baby. Overall, the nurses just had a great welcoming atmosphere.

At one point, I was alone to gather my thoughts. All of a sudden, I hear a nurse yell, "Left, left!" Lo and behold, it was my mom! The nurse just happened to be walking by and I started laughing. I told her that's hilarious because she was a teacher!

The nurse laughs and says, "Oh my gosh!" and pretends to be a parent calling about not knowing left from right. Mom laughs and explains she was getting lost on the way here.

I laughed and told the nurse, "You know what her nickname is? Magoo!"

The nurse laughs and says, "Oh my gosh, she is like that episode when he goes through the construction site like nothing."

My mom and I laughed at the Magoo joke, and it felt good to laugh before surgery to ease my nerves. Prior to meeting the surgeon, Dr. Brown, I learned that he is extremely precise and completed fourteen thousand port placements and loves to sing during surgery. Later, Dr. Brown came into the room to introduce himself. He seemed so much like an introvert; you wouldn't suspect him to sing in front of complete strangers. They roll me over to the surgery room, and I see white walls and huge machines with lights that hover above your head.

As I proceed to the operating table, they tell me, "Okay, we are going to begin." The music comes on, and he begins to sing! At first I thought, *Oh gosh, this is crazy!* Later as it went on, it was nice to hear music, and the sedatives did the trick in relaxing me. I even fell asleep during the procedure, woke up at one point, and Dr. Brown was still singing. At first, I remembered the song, but as time went on, I couldn't remember.

Later that evening, I received an email from Dr. Brown that included all his songs from his website. I thank him for a memorable experience for my first surgery. It was actually a pleasant experience, as strange as that sounds.

My sweet loves, this was a strange yet pleasant experience. God places people in our paths that help us or teach us life lessons. The best thing we can do is continue to love one another.

> God is love, and anyone who doesn't love
> others has never known him. (1 John 4:8 CEV)

> Instead, be kind and merciful, and forgive
> others, just as God forgave you because of Christ.
> (Ephesians 4:32 CEV)

Second Chemotherapy Treatment

Going back to MD Anderson, I feel like I'm in a better place mentally. I know it's keeping me alive and from spreading because drugs are doing their job. Once we arrived home, I texted my mom to please give me a buzz cut because the hair was falling out. I had a huge chunk that was matted, and I couldn't take the fallout anymore. Mom said she prayed as she proceeded to shave my hair off. I just felt a sense of relief; my head felt hot and sometimes itchy from the dead patches.

As I saw all the hair in the trash can, part of me still can't believe that I'm going through this. My mind sometimes believes that I don't have my illness. I'm not some fragile person bedridden. I just feel like I still have so much even with this illness. Lately, it seems that I've been reading about the deaths of people taken too soon. I'm still here with limbs and mind intact. How can I not consider this a blessing? I remind myself, keep the faith and press forward by the grace of God.

Rebekah's father-in-law has been dealing with a recent diagnosis of tongue cancer. I send her messages of hope and prayers, and I tell her that I'm praying for him. When she sent the message about one of the stress tests coming back abnormal, it hit me. I just felt a tear streaming down my face. Cancer is a beast, and I just immediately prayed, "Lord, my God, please don't let this be so. God of miracles, send peace and strength to get through so he can have the surgery."

My daughter Melanie ends up falling asleep at my side, and as I leave, I just can't shake this feeling. I sat up in my bed, crying out to God and saying, "This sickness, Lord, why must we endure?" As I'm crying, I just thank him for giving me time with my family and that I rebuke this cancer in his name.

My precious loves, we will go through hills and valleys in this life. Emotionally, I was fine on some days. Other days, not so much. The only way I was able to push through those tough times was by reminding myself over and over to keep the faith, even if I felt that I had nothing left. Listening to music of hope and faith was my constant comfort.

Let your hope make you glad. Be patient in
time of trouble and never stop praying. (Romans
12:12 CEV)

Battlefield of the Mind

Years ago, I read a book titled *Battlefield of the Mind* by Joyce Meyer. It was about understanding how our thoughts have a profound impact on our lives and how the enemy robs us of our bond with God. Looking back, I realized that was a prep read for what I was going to endure. I consider myself a strong person, but this is an entire level of strength beyond me. The only reason I've been able to endure is God's grace and peace. The moment I learned about my cancer diagnosis, I prayed for peace in my heart. I knew I had a choice between being bitter or being content for what I've got. When we were on the way back from my diagnosis with the doctor, my dear friend Vanesa stated, "The mind is a powerful thing and controls everything."

She is correct, and her reminder made me understand that I needed to be aware of my thoughts and stand firm in my faith. I'm a strong person, my friend Rebekah tells me. I tell her and Vanesa, "Girls, I'm an overachiever and I've got no choice. I've got to do this for them."

How can my family not be all the motivation I need? My family is everything, more than words can ever express. I'm not going to say it has been a breeze every day. I've got my dark moments, but I try to pray about it and ask God to help me because I want to be a testimony!

I've read many beautiful devotionals, and here is one that was just what I needed to be reminded of. God knows what we need! This is from *The Six Truths of Motherhood* by Karen Stubbs:

> "There are two choices in life, we can hold
> onto resentment or rest in the fact that God

can be trusted. We can trust that God works all things for good for those that love him. (Romans 8:28) Living a resentful, bitter life is no way to live. A restful spirit is a better choice. Choose rest today."

After Port Placement

After the port placement, I feel soreness and a happy feeling—like I'm moving forward to getting better. Chemo was better for me, and I'm grateful there are no real symptoms to keep me from living. My girls are happy to spend time with their grandparents, and that makes me happy deep in my soul. Being ill with two small children—three and one—is no easy feat. I'm so grateful to have my parents at my side. I feel like a kid again at times, but now with kids of my own—and with my parents, it can feel strange at times. I'm looking forward to my sister's wedding and feeling grateful in general, but I'm also sad that I'm dealing with all this. Keep moving forward is all I can do.

> I patiently waited, LORD, for you to hear my prayer. You listened and pulled me from a lonely pit full of mud and mire. You let me stand on a rock with my feet firm, and you gave me a new song, a song of praise to you. Many will see this, and they will honor and trust you, the LORD God. (Psalms 40:1–3 CEV)

Mind Games

Throughout this process, I can honestly say my peace from God has pulled me through. Today was the hardest day by far. I guess when my mom talks about trips or traveling, it makes me sad or even angry. How can I see past my illness? I feel that just making it to another Christmas is a blessing and my goal. My plans for the future seem to be smaller, and sometimes it's just a hard feeling to brave a life cut short with plans derailed and dreams gone.

Depressing, yes it can be. I just had to leave the room and cry in the restroom. I thought, *Why, Lord? How much more?* I just found myself asking for peace in my head and all those thoughts to just leave my mind. I sat down, took deep breaths, and just asked God for peace and to vanish the negativity. I'm still here and thankful to be with my family, even if it hurts sometimes to hear future plans. *Trust, Sarah, trust in him*—that is what I continue to pray.

Here is a devotional reading from Billy Graham's book *Hope for Each Day: Words of Wisdom and Faith* (January 2, page 3, "The Sun Still Shining").

> They looked…and behold, the glory of the LORD appeared in the cloud. (Exodus 16:10)

> "Without the clouds we wouldn't be shielded from the burning sun. Without the clouds there would be no lavish sunsets, no beneficial rain, no beautiful landscapes.

The same is true with life's clouds. When hard times come, we easily get discouraged. But behind the clouds God is still present, and can even use them to water our souls with unexpected blessings. Longfellow once wrote, "Be still, sad heart, and cease repining; behind the clouds is the sun still shining." As God's people wandered in the wilderness, He declared, "Behold, I come to you in the thick cloud." (Exodus 19:9)

Each of us experiences clouds in life-sometimes slight, but sometimes dark and frightening. Whatever clouds you face today, ask Jesus, the light of the world, to help you look behind the cloud to see His glory and His plans for you."

Wedding Day

Today is my little sister's wedding day. Happiness all around, but also a bit of sadness as I'm reminded of my illness by wearing my wig. My family tells me it looks natural; I just have to accept that this is part of the process. I'm able to attend, and I'm feeling good: no aches, pains, or symptoms. Blessings all around, and I'm grateful. I wonder if my new brother-in-law told some relatives of my diagnosis. Regardless, I'll stick to wearing a mask. The wedding ceremony and reception was beautiful. I'm glad I got to see my relatives and thank them for the prayers.

Awkward to speak about it at such a joyous occasion, but I understand why they wanted to share their feelings about it. No one in our family has dealt with this, and I pray this doesn't happen to anyone in the family ever! It is interesting to hear my family talk about being brave and positive. Negativity will get us out of nowhere, and God doesn't want us living that way.

I refuse to be depressed and would rather see each day as a blessing to be with my family. Doing the most mundane chores, I'm thankful for the ability to continue living like I don't have cancer! Living with cancer is the hardest thing I've ever dealt with in my life, but what a beautiful life I've lived so far. Precious memories and the sweet girls that I know are going to do better in every aspect. Each generation gets better, and they are going to outdo their parents.

My precious beauties, we had a beautiful day at the wedding of your Aunt Sandra and Uncle Eric. We got to dance a bit and hear beautiful live music. I'm so thankful I was able to share that experience with you. During the ceremony, the priest talked about love. It's not the love we like to think about here on Earth; the Bible talks about love as eternal…God's love.

> Love is patient and kind, never jealous, boastful, proud, or rude. Love isn't selfish or quick tempered. It doesn't keep a record of wrongs that others do. Love rejoices in the truth, but not in evil. Love is always supportive, loyal, hopeful, and trusting. Love never fails! (1 Corinthians 13:4–8 CEV)

To Laugh Again

Completed the second round of chemo, and by the grace of God, I'm feeling good days after.

I'm getting ready for my third round with my father and step-mother accompanying me. Physically, it has been good. Emotionally, I've had some rough days, but I just try to cast out those thoughts of fear and doubt from the enemy. During the time I was at my father's house, I had a horrible nightmare—I was lying down, yelling with a black mist leaving my mouth. I awoke and immediately prayed and read scriptures.

The following day, I mentioned the dream to my father. He asked when I had the dream because the other night, he felt strange—like a bad feeling. I said to my dad, "Did you pray?"

He said, "Yes, and I ended up falling asleep again."

I can't help feeling like the enemy is just trying to attack, and so I continued to pray and ask God for protection, peace, and healing. Later that night, I arrived back home and woke up at a strange hour in the night. I prayed and just said, "Lord, if you need me, I will go to you. If you don't need me, I will be your testimony for my family, friends, and those I come across in my life."

The following day, my daughter got her Happy Meal from McDonald's as a Friday treat. The prize happened to be a box of Disney Mickey memory cards. I joked with my parents that we should play. I ended up playing with my dad, and I lost! My step-mom played with me, and I also lost. My stepmom and I played three times, and on the third time, we were both forgetting where things were and picked the wrong cards. We laughed so hard that my dad came out of the bedroom as he was trying to put my daughter Natalie to sleep. He said he could hear the laughter. I haven't had a good laugh like that, the kind of laugh where tears come out, in so long. Interestingly, days later, I read a podcast title that says, "You're going to laugh again." I just read that and smiled.

Precious loves, there will be days when it feels like things will not get better. During my career as a teacher, there were some tough times. I didn't think I could make it through another year. I ended up completing thirteen years before my cancer diagnosis. Your Grandma Gigi always would tell me, "This too shall pass," and it does.

> I come to you, LORD, for protection.
> Don't let me be ashamed. Do as you have prom-
> ised and rescue me.
> Listen to my prayer
> and hurry to save me. Be my mighty rock and the
> fortress where I am safe. You, LORD God,
> are my mighty rock and my fortress.
> Lead me and guide me, so that your name will
> be honored.
> Protect me from hidden traps and keep me safe.
> You are faithful, and I trust you
> because you rescued me. (Psalms 31: 1–5 CEV)

Only God

My dad and stepmom accompanied me for another MD Anderson appointment. I was nervous for them because it can be overwhelming to be in a facility surrounded by hospitals. Thankfully, all went well and my dad came back in better spirits. I cried hearing some news about going in for a follow-up because I thought it was bad news from my MRI brain scan. The nurse called me back to clarify that my MRI came back with no lesions or progression; it was stable. My tears just came out like a flood. I scared my parents and, through my tears, shared that it was good news.

My dad cried and just held me saying, "You're my little girl, and coming to MD Anderson, I know you're in good hands. I've been praying, and you've been so strong and positive. My gosh, you're the strongest person I know, with everything you've accomplished and with your girls."

I told my dad, "Grandma had so much faith, and they were such great examples. I have to be strong for the girls and Randy [my husband]."

After some tears, we calmed down and I prayed in the restroom. Down on my knees, I thanked God for all he has done even though I don't deserve his mercy. I know it is all him. God, that's healing me. I said, "Thank you with all my heart and soul. I can never repay you. I know you are helping me keep my faith and have peace in my heart."

Cancer will change you, but I feel this is only changing me for the better. My faith is at its strongest, and this is, by far, the most difficult trial in my life. God does miracles, and only he can. Thank you, God.

Precious beauties, this was difficult for everyone. Cancer not only affects the person, but also the family. There are countless stories of survivors and those who continue to live regardless of the circumstances. I may be broken inside this body, but I still have a fighting spirit. The days are not always easy, but I practice gratitude and thank God for another day.

> With all my heart I praise the LORD, and with all that I am I praise his holy name! With all my heart I praise the LORD! I will never forget how kind he has been. The LORD forgives our sins, heals us when we are sick, and protects us from death. His kindness and love are a crown on our heads. Each day that we live, he provides for our needs and gives us the strength of a young eagle. (Psalms 103:1–5 CEV)

Living

After my third chemo treatment, I continued to practice gratitude, prayer, faith, and patience. I spent a couple of days at my dad's house to ensure I get rest and have normalcy for the girls. Going to the local park and beach was so great for all of us. I reminded myself that despite this disease, I'm still here to enjoy these days with my family and feeling good physically. I am able to continue my daily activities, and that is a blessing. Do I have fear creeping in? Absolutely. I ask God to help me cast out those thoughts and enjoy time with my family.

Sometimes at night, this becomes difficult. The mind doesn't rest, and neither do those negative thoughts. Tears in my eyes, I just pray and ask God for forgiveness, mercy, and healing. Praying for family and friends, gratitude, and continued peace. Devotionals, prayers, and encouraging words from others like Mrs. Vivian Deanda have helped me through difficult nights. Thankfully, I slept soundly while my dad and stepmom helped me with my girls. To all the mothers with young children, dealing with this disease is beyond words, but we continue to fight for them.

My precious beauties, surround yourself with positive people. In this life, you will meet many people, and one thing I've learned during my journey is to take lessons to heart. We learn from each other how bitterness destroys the soul and how joyful people convey themselves. We have a lot to be joyful for, so always choose joy!

So put on all the armor that God gives.
Then when that evil day comes, you will be able

to defend yourself. And when the battle is over, you will still be standing firm.

Be ready! Let the truth be like a belt around your waist, and let God's justice protect you like armor. Your desire to tell the good news about peace should be like shoes on your feet. Let your faith be like a shield, and you will be able to stop all the flaming arrows of the evil one. Let God's saving power be like a helmet, and for a sword use God's message that comes from the Spirit. (Ephesians 6:13–17 CEV)

Friends

A big part of your cancer journey is your friends. My friends are the best people. I'm a private person, and I don't just have anyone be part of my life. I've known these friends for over ten years or more through college or my first job. They have seen me go through life stages with marriage and kids. They have been my biggest supporters throughout this journey. We smile at each other under the circumstances, and I thank God they have continued to be in my life.

My girlfriends and I had a little gathering, and I told them that I am forever changed. How can cancer not change you? They looked at me with bewilderment, but also with understanding of how it has affected my family. I told them about prayer and how my husband is coping. In the end, we can't wait for this season to be over; and God willing, it will be a distant memory so we can move forward as a family forever changed in so many ways.

My sweet girls, friends will come and go, but some friendships will last. They say in times of trouble, you find out who your true friends are. I've been blessed to have wonderful friends, and I hope you will have great friendships in adulthood.

> This is why you must encourage and help each other, just as you are already doing. (1 Thessalonians 5:11 CEV)

Put up with each other, and forgive anyone who does you wrong, just as Christ has forgiven you. (Colossians 3:13 CEV)

If you fall, your friend can help you up. But if you fall without having a friend nearby, you are really in trouble. (Ecclesiastes 4:10 CEV)

Peaceful Days

Although there are times of sorrow, I'm grateful for the days with my family when I can continue daily routines even if I sometimes feel like a walking disease. Cancer is strange; it is a constant battlefield of the mind because I'm so good physically, but internally, it's a different story. My mind will sometimes be like, *I don't have anything*, and then it will hit me: *Oh yeah, cancer!*

I feel like I'm trying to make the most out of this madness, even though by the grace of God, I've been good throughout treatments. I can't believe I'll be getting my fourth treatment. I'm not the same person mentally and spiritually. I didn't look at mundane things the same way—laundry, dishes, taking care of my girls. I was transitioning to being a stay-at-home mom when I got diagnosed, and it was tough for an independent person like me. I worked for thirteen years and earned my own pay, and even though the job was stressful, the students kept me going.

Teaching is still in my soul, and I hope to get back to it. I'm going to get a PET scan to see any progress. My hope is for the best, but like what I cried from the very beginning, I'm just saying, "Lord, it's out of my hands. Your will be done."

My sweet girls, this is by far the most difficult thing I've gone through in my life. The choice for me to stay home with you was exciting and overwhelming at the same time. I was saddened that we had to stay buckled down at home due to COVID-19, and then there's my chemo treatments. We would make the best of staying home by singing songs, reading books, listening to music, watching movies, coloring, painting, and playing outside. I was grateful that you weren't sick and continued to be happy children. Here is a reading from a devotional that helped me put things in perspective. This is from *Take Hold of the Faith You Long For* by Sharon Jaynes:

> "If you are waiting to feel unafraid before moving forward, you most likely never will. Being brave and living bold does not mean you won't be afraid. It means you move forward in faith even though you still are. It means you kick fear out the door with courage and walk past it, out into this big, wonderful world."

Good News

Making another trip to Houston, I'm in good spirits overall despite feeling nervous. The PET scan went well, and they received a new machine that was extremely quiet. The technician even noted that it is taking pictures although it is quiet, so I need to be very still. My arms are over my head so they can get the best results they need.

Before the scan, I was put in a room so that the medication could run throughout the body. I look at the beautiful pond with an abundant variety of flowers. As I stare at it, I suddenly remember the scripture Matthew 6:26 which says, "Look at the birds of the air; they do not sow or reap or store away in barns, and yet your heavenly Father feeds them. Are you not much more valuable than they?"

As I sat there waiting for the medication to settle, I began to look for a bird. I didn't find one, so I began to feel disappointed. However, looking at the picture again, I found one bird standing on a stick near the end of the pond. I just thought, *God, you are taking care of me through all of this.*

The following day, I had bloodwork, doctor visitation, and chemotherapy treatment. Thankfully, while I was waiting for the doctor, Nurse McCarthy comes in with papers. My heart begins to race as she says, "Okay, I've got good news and good news!"

My heart just burst; I didn't even know how to react. She begins reading the results and stating how my results show that I'm nearly cancer-free in my breast and lymph nodes, completely clear on bone. I've got a tiny spot in the lung, but that is clearing up as well.

Through tears, I was just thanking God. I gave Nurse McCarthy a hug and thanked her for the support.

Later, Dr. Valero came in and spoke about the good news. He wanted to share my bloodwork with me. In a sense, he couldn't explain how the results ended up like that. *God, this is all you*—that was all I thought in my head. As Dr. Valero left, he gave me a big hug. He was happy for me.

I shared the news with family and friends. I'm continuing my journey until I'm 100 percent cancer-free! The medical team was happy for me—so happy that for the rest of the day, they shared good news to other patients. I hope and pray there is more happy news.

My loves, this day was full of tears and gratitude toward God. We had so many people praying for me, and we knew this great news was a result of all those prayers. I just thought that I now have more time to spend with you girls as well as your father. It made my heart full.

This is a reading from a devotional from YouVersion, "Overcomer: Finding Strength in Hard Seasons," day 3:

> "Whatever you're facing, God has a perfect record of turning broken hopes and dreams around for our good and His glory. He has never stopped working in your life. No matter what hardships you face, God will continue to show you favor and love when you continue to walk with Him.
>
> And when you walk with God, nothing you go through is wasted."

Home

My family was happy to hear the news. Life seemed a little brighter, and I felt so relieved that my girls will one day know all that I and their father went through. I can only hope so many others get good news from this horrible disease. For now, I am enjoying and treasuring everything, from the birds and the sky to my family and even the mundane things.

My loves, I was happy to have good news, and things seemed to be brighter. I pray that you don't need a brick in your life to make you appreciate things in life. Here is the story of The Brick. I learned this story from your Grandpa Morales during one of his sermons. The story goes like this:

"A young and successful executive was traveling down a neighborhood street, going a bit too fast in his new Jaguar. He was watching for kids darting out from between parked cars and slowed down when he thought he saw something.

As his car passed, no children appeared. Instead, a brick smashed into the Jag's side door! He slammed on the brakes and backed the Jag back to the spot where the brick had been thrown. The angry driver then jumped out of the car, grabbed the nearest kid, and pushed him up against a parked car shouting, "What was that all about and who are you? Just what the heck are you doing? That's a new car and that brick you threw is going to cost a lot of money. Why did you do it?"

The young boy was apologetic. "Please, mister…please! I'm sorry, but I didn't know what else to do," he pleaded. "I threw the brick because no one else would stop…"

With tears dripping down his face and off his chin, the youth pointed to a spot just around a parked car. "It's my brother," he said. "He rolled off the curb and fell out of his wheelchair, and I can't lift him up."

Now sobbing, the boy asked the stunned executive, "Would you please help me get him back into his wheelchair? He's hurt and he's too heavy for me."

Moved beyond words, the driver tried to swallow the rapidly swelling lump in his throat. He hurriedly lifted the handicapped boy back into the wheelchair, then he took out a linen handkerchief and dabbed it on the fresh scrapes and cuts. A quick look told him everything was going to be okay.

"Thank you, and may God bless you," the grateful child told the stranger.

Too shook up for words, the man simply watched the boy push his wheelchair-bound brother down the sidewalk toward their home.

It was a long, slow walk back to the Jaguar. The damage was very noticeable, but the driver never bothered to repair the dented side door. He kept the dent there to remind him of this message: don't go through life so fast that someone has to throw a brick at you to get your attention!

God whispers in our souls and speaks to our hearts. Sometimes, when we don't have time to listen, he has to throw a brick at us. It's our choice to listen or not."— Author Unknown

Fifth Treatment

The Sugarland location was just for chemotherapy. I told my daughter Melanie that it was a quick trip and didn't even mention the doctor. I'm so thankful my family is in good health and that my parents are so helpful. My daughters couldn't be in better hands.

I've been feeling relief after seeing some signs of finishing chemo treatment. I napped pretty well after all the things, but the good thing is that I feel good when I wake up. I know that not everyone responds well to chemo, so I'm beyond grateful for the ability to continue normalcy in life.

Speaking of normalcy, the day we arrived in Sugarland, we stopped for lunch at Pappasitos. They didn't want to use the outdoor area, so my husband says, "Oh we wanted to use it because my wife is going through chemotherapy."

I was like, *Wow, he actually told them.* We sat outside. Part of me was sad about it, and the other was relieved because it can be a wake-up call for young people.

Precious loves, we have a tendency to get lost in the way of the world. We tend to think success is a big house and nice car. Once you obtain those things, you will want more things, and the cycle of being unsatisfied continues. You need to look at the overall picture of how wonderful life is and thank God for all he has done. Practice gratitude every day. This is a reading from a devotional from Spikenard, "Anchorage: The Seven Storms Overview," part 1 of 8, day 2:

"The more I reflect and sit in the beauty of nature, the more I realize the wisdom of Jesus's use of everyday sights to bring peace. Think about it. How common is it to see birds whirring through the air? Whenever you see them, you're reminded of Jesus's words about the sparrows. They are in the Father's care. They don't toil, but they're fed and thriving. And what about the trees that bring shade to protect you from the scorching heat? His mercies are built into the atmosphere to reveal His protection and peace.

It's easy to feel peace on that park bench, but, I get it—some moments in life are not park-bench experiences. When the sirens wail, the wind bends the trees, and rain floods in, the question remains: How do we tap into peace in the midst of chaos? (Philippians 4:6–7)

It's safe to say that a conversation with God and intentional gratefulness are a part of the answer. We'd be shocked to see how our mind transforms with these two practices."

Don't worry about anything, but pray about everything. With thankful hearts offer up your prayers and requests to God. (Philippians 4:6–7 CEV)

Easter Sunday Testimony

When your father asked me if I wanted to share my testimony, I just thought, *God, this is for you.* I had no trouble writing it out on my phone; the words just seem to flow out partly because it's my experience with God.

In December 2022, I was diagnosed with stage 3 inflammatory breast cancer—a rare cancer that occurs in women under forty, according to the American Cancer Society. Cancer occurs in stages: stages 1 to 3 which, with treatment, are curable; and then stage 4 which is incurable. Once, when I sought a second opinion for treatment, I was diagnosed with stage 4. My supportive husband reminded me that if anyone can get through this, it's me.

At thirty-eight, cancer left me feeling a variety of emotions—mostly sadness for my family. I knew that once I left the doctor's office, I had two choices: I could either let despair take over and steal my joy, or I could surrender to God and keep the faith.

Surrender did not come easy for me, and there were several nights of tears, thoughts of fear, and questioning my ability to endure chemo treatments while taking care of my two girls. How can you find joy through a dark season in life?

Pray first! My friends Rebekah and Vanesa gave me an inspirational gift that I placed on my kitchen window seal stating the following words from Philippians 4:6 NLT: "Don't worry about anything; instead, pray about everything. Tell God what you need, and thank him for all he has done."

I prayed several times throughout the day for strength and peace in my heart. I dealt with a battlefield of the mind at times, having moments of doubt and fear. I would pray to the Lord to cast these thoughts out of my mind.

Late one night, with tears in my eyes, I prayed to the Lord, "If you need me to go with you I will, but if I stay, I will share my testimony with as many people as I can. Your will be done, Lord."

The next months, I continued to read devotionals and scriptures and prayed for continued peace, strength, and healing.

I read one scripture that addressed worry. This is from Luke 12:22–26 NIV:

> Then Jesus said to his disciples, "Therefore I tell you, do not worry about your life, what you will eat; or about your body, what you will wear. For life is more than food, and the body more than clothes. Consider the ravens: They do not sow or reap, they have no storeroom or barn; yet God feeds them. And how much more valuable you are than birds! Who of you by worrying can add a single hour to your life? Since you cannot do this very little thing, why do you worry about the rest?

Those particular verses stuck with me. During my next visit, I was getting a full-body PET scan to see how I've been responding after three chemo treatments. I was put in a small room to wait for an hour to allow the medicine to go throughout the body. Each room has a lighted picture of nature to look at while you wait. While waiting, I was looking at it and thought, *What a beautiful place!*

After staring at it, I suddenly stumbled upon a bird standing on a branch above the pond. I immediately remembered the Matthew 6:25 (ISV) verse, "You are more valuable than they are, aren't you?" I felt an enormous sense of peace and a divine reminder that everything is in God's hands.

The following day, I was up for my fourth chemo treatment. By God's grace, I've been responding with minor side effects that allowed me to carry on with daily activities and keep up with my two little girls.

I was waiting for a follow-up with my doctor to address the scan results before continuing with further treatment. The results were in. My doctor told me, "Which news do you want? I have good news and good news." My results show very good response to the treatment. Nearly cancer-free in my breast and lymph nodes. Completely clear on bone, only a small spot on the lung but even that is clearing up as well. My doctor says he is very pleased and that I am improving faster than the typical patient.

He is only recommending six treatments and after that, I'll stop chemo treatment to begin the anti-therapy pill.

Thanks be to God, I though, and there were many tears of joy and hugs. Praising God is all I thought of when the doctor left. I told the nurse practitioner that it's five things for me: God, faith, family, friends, and a positive attitude.

Laughing, the nurse says, "Oh, we are the sixth."

I told her that to be here at MD Anderson was part of God's plan.

It is only because of God's great mercy and grace that I have made it through the darkest season of my life. I am a witness of his power, and I will never be the same. I pray differently and acquired a different perspective on life, and my faith has only deepened. God can change your life if you allow him to, just keep believing beyond your circumstances and stand your ground in faith.

Journey Continues

B efore treatment, a small spot on my brain was found, but it was stable. They found that the spot grew a bit, and a tiny puncture appeared on the left side. They recommended radiation and explained the process to me. Nerves kicked in, but I knew that God helped me before. The lesions are small, and this will get rid of those spots. I cried and got on my knees and prayed to God, thanking him for all that he has done. He will get me through this like he did in the past. I will continue to pray for strength and peace in my heart as I go through this process.

My loves, I was saddened to hear of my diagnosis. However, I knew that God had helped me through this journey. I continue to fight and make the best of my time.

Music is good for the soul, and I hope you find comfort in songs of hope and faith in God.

Radiation

Here at the hotel again for treatment in Houston, I'm feeling anxious because I want it over with. My prayer is for a one-time treatment and for it to be done. Praying for good news from another PET scan.

After the results from brain MRI, I was a bit shaken—my mind was going a bit toward doubt. However, by the grace of God and friends' prayers, I'm feeling more at peace.

My precious girls, there will be times in this life when you will have to go out of your comfort zone. I pray you never have to experience this disease and all that it entails. God can give you the perseverance to deal with your struggles, just pray for strength.

> Let your hope make you glad. Be patient in time of trouble and never stop praying. (Romans 12:12 CEV)

Results

After the radiation and PET scan, I was beginning to feel like a lab rat. I'm glad that God gave me the strength to complete the tests. During the brain MRI, I had a vision of Rebekah's parents. They were happy in heaven as angels so pure and as the brightest light. I wanted to cry, but I held my composure because I was getting scanned. I messaged Rebekah after the scan, and she was happy to learn how beautiful it was. She misses her parents every day.

My PET scan results were good, and by the grace of God, cancer didn't spread around. I've got to continue the fight; they did see a little spot in the breast area and would like to continue through the eighth treatment. However, I should complete my last treatment on May 30. I just keep my darling girls in my heart and remember how much they need me. My husband continues fighting the journey with me, helping my mind keep thinking positive, and praying for me.

My precious beauties, I can't even begin to explain how my friend's parents looked during the scan. I don't know how they came to my mind. They looked so beautiful and happy. I just felt so much joy when I saw them; it brought tears to my eyes. We dare to imagine what heaven will be like, but it is beyond what we could even fathom. How great is our God!

> How great is God's love for all who worship him?
> Greater than the distance between heaven and
> earth! How far has the LORD taken our sins from us?
> Farther than the distance from east to west!

Just as parents are kind
to their children, the LORD is kind
to all who worship him, because he knows we are
made of dust.
We humans are like grass or wild flowers
that quickly bloom. (Psalms 103:11–15 CEV)

Perseverance

I am not who I was since my diagnosis. I've changed my diet, my faith has grown stronger, and I'm grateful for the little things. Dare I say, sometimes I wake up thinking that I don't have cancer only to realize the opposite. I mostly have good days, but I have my moments of sadness when I start to think, *When will this end?* I long for normalcy and try to enjoy outings with my daughters. I'm getting tired of this whole process, but I have to remember who I'm fighting for because it helps keep me going.

My sweet girls, patience is one of the hardest things to endure. In such a fast-paced world, we want things done in an instant. God doesn't work on our time; we don't know what he is protecting us from or what may be better for us. In the end, it does work out for good. How do I know? I've experienced it for myself. I've always told myself that I wouldn't teach at a junior-high level. When I didn't get the job at my old elementary where I taught for several years, I was a bit hurt. However, I ended up in a wonderful school environment and loved junior high! I met amazing people and had wonderful parental support. You see girls, God didn't want me back at my old campus—he had something better for me!

This devotional is from "Trusting God's Plan in the Waiting: Lessons from the Life of Joseph" by HealingStrong. This is from "Day 4: The Lord Was with Joseph."

"Bloom where you are planted. Ever heard
of that phrase? Simply put, make the most of

where God has you RIGHT NOW, even in your season of waiting. This doesn't mean you have to like your situation, but your attitude in it makes all the difference! Why? Because you have an audience watching how you live your life, as we see in Joseph's story."

Precious Moments

B eing at home, my family and I have been watching some movies. Disney movies always seem to have someone die. My daughter Melanie always seems to comment, "Ooh, they died."

I can't help but think about my own life. I don't want my family to experience a funeral at such a young age and my daughters to lose their mother. I just ask God to please help me see my girls grow up because I know they need their mother. I've had some weird moments where I'm fine and then I'll just start shedding tears thinking about my situation. Cancer is so cruel because it is a lengthy, ongoing process. Sometimes, I just have to breathe, pray, and cry out to God to help me with these thoughts of anxiety. I message my friend Maria later that day, and she responds in such a touching way. This is her text:

> Aww girl! I can understand how we can feel sadness in our life especially when we are dealing with health issues. This morning when I was driving my daughter to her last day of school, I was a little teary eyed. I'm like, "My gosh how time has passed by?" And I thanked God for letting me see another day! I also prayed to him to give you and me the opportunity to see our children graduate high school, college and see them live a happy life! I was thinking about you this morning. Everyday I think about you and pray for you. I know our journeys that we are

traveling on are not easy for us at this moment,
but God only knows why we are having to endure
this path in our lives 😔 🙏!

Tears just flood my eyes as I'm walking and reading her message. We lean on each other because we know what it's like to have an illness that can take your life. I know a big reason why I'm here is for my family; they need me and I need them. No life is perfect and exempt from pain.

My precious loves, there are times that we get so consumed about the "what ifs" that we lose focus on the present. Life is a gift, and the best defense against the enemy is to pray and surrender our burdens. My hope is that you remember to turn to God during your "what if" moments. I received many messages of encouragement during this process. Here is one from Mrs. Vivian:

So glad you are doing well. Our mind is so powerful. When it goes against the word of God we need to take our thoughts captive to be obedient to what the word of God tells us in our situations. By His stripes you are healed. Don't let your mind stray from that. He said it and it is true. He cannot lie. Keep thoughts away by proclaiming what God said. 💞

Eighth Chemotherapy Treatment

Going back to MD Anderson, I feel a bit of relief knowing that it may be my last round of chemotherapy. I'm so grateful to have minimal side effects. My father and stepmother came along with me this time. I feel sad, anxious, and relieved all at the same time. We try to make the best of these trips by eating at different places and trying different foods. My treatment is late in the afternoon, so we have time to chat. We take our time during lunch. It turned out to be a nice day to sit outside, so we did. During our chatter, I received a call from the doctor to see if we can do our Zoom call earlier. I said, "Sure, no problem."

Later that day, I went in for chemotherapy. Overall, the nurses have been awesome. For this last time, I have two male nurses. One jokes and says, "We are divorcing today."

I look at him like, *what?* I just laugh and say, "Oh yeah, didn't think of it that way." I always feel at ease knowing I'm in good hands. As the nurse gets me prepped, I pray in my head, *Lord, help me through.*

My loves, you need to choose joy in the midst of trials. Don't let the bitterness of your situation affect those around you. I've witnessed what bitterness does to the soul, and it destroys. I've tried my best every day to remember that my cancer is not my fault nor anyone else's. God doesn't give us more than what we can bear, even though it feels beyond our capabilities.

Another Wedding

Another joyous occasion—this time, my nephew's wedding. My feelings are of sadness and gratefulness. My parents took my eldest daughter to the ceremony. Later, we all went together to the reception. My daughter's first experience was my sister's wedding, so I was happy to see my girls experience it again. As the night wore on, I wore my mask due to my chemotherapy treatment three days prior. I made the best of it by dancing with my daughters since their father was out of town finishing up graduate school.

As I watched the bride dance with her mother due to her father's passing, it made me sad. I may not see my girls get married. I also felt for the newlyweds; this life can be so heartbreaking with hills and valleys in life. I hope they never experience an illness like this.

Our eleventh anniversary is coming up in the same month. Looking back, neither of us ever thought cancer would end up in my life. We can try to question God, but we will never understand his ways—and that's okay. Perhaps we are not supposed to understand. All I can do is live the best life for my family, and I intend to continue to do just that.

My precious loves, what a joyous occasion for us all! I was happy that we got to spend this time together at your cousin's wedding. I pray someday you will find the one God has for you. I knew in my soul that your father was the one for me. I've always had high standards even while dating; I just wouldn't settle for less. I just knew in my heart that I wanted to have a marriage that lasts forever and break the cycle of divorce. God turned that around for good, because there is so much love around for you girls with three sets of grandparents!

> Love each other with genuine affection, and take delight in honoring each other. (Romans 12:10 NLT)

Melanie's Birthday

My firstborn Melanie turns four today; the years really do go by so quickly. I'm grateful to be in good spirits and feeling well. My parents and I pick her up from vocational Bible school and head to Peter Piper Pizza for a little celebration. My sister joins us, and we have a good time playing games and eating. My heart was overjoyed watching Melanie blow out her candles. We plan to have another celebration with both sides of the family soon. My father and stepmom also have a surprise birthday planned for her too when we visit. I'm so thankful that she is surrounded by so much love. The only reason I've made it this far is because of love, God's love, friends, and family. Today was just a sweet day and I'm grateful.

My sweet girls, today was a joyous occasion and even in the midst of the storm, there was peace. I listened to many beautiful songs that reminded me of God's peace.

Pray that our LORD will make us strong
and give us peace. (Psalms 29:11 CEV)

Old Friends

You know, it's strange letting people know my diagnosis, especially if I haven't seen them or kept in touch in a while. Friendships get hard to maintain due to jobs, family, and life. I find myself saddened to let them know, but there is some relief because I've come a long way—and by God's grace, I'm doing well. God has a way of putting people in your life, and sometimes, they may turn up again out of the blue when you least expect it.

My loves, I treasure those lasting friendships and I have so many wonderful memories with my friends. During this process, my friends were with me to lift me up through my darkest moments. I pray that you have wonderful people in your life to lean on and make beautiful memories.

There is a beautiful song on friendship, written and sung by Carole King. James Taylor also did a nice cover of the song that my dad would listen to often.

Melanie's Birthday

My daughter celebrated her birthday again with family and her godparents. We decided to rent a bounce house, and it was a great choice. My daughter loved spending time with her cousins and opening up her gifts. Surprisingly, she decided to give us a little demonstration of a dance she learned at vocational Bible school. I was so elated to see my daughter break out of her shell. I was so grateful to see my beautiful girl celebrate another birthday in good health, and with such joy. Regardless of what happens to me in the future, I have faith that she will be in God's good hands.

> I kneel in prayer to the Father. All beings in heaven and on earth receive their life from him. God is wonderful and glorious. I pray that his Spirit will make you become strong followers and that Christ will live in your hearts because of your faith. Stand firm and be deeply rooted in his love. (Ephesians 3:14–18 CEV)

Father's Day

Today we celebrated your dad. I'm glad you have a wonderful father, and I know he will continue to love you with all his heart every step of the way in your life. Please be gentle with your father. When you both were little, you were very attached to him to the point where he couldn't put you down without crying. I learned that your dad was very attached to his father when he was a baby.

Your father has been so supportive during this whole process, and it has been the hardest thing we have gone through as a family. We couldn't have imagined that in saying our vows in sickness and health, it meant that I would be fighting cancer. My hope is one day, you will have that kind of support from your husband during your time of need.

My precious loves, your father has been very supportive during this entire process. He remained so strong even though he may have felt the opposite. I felt so much peace when he would pray over me, and he even asked for prayer from church elders. Through it all, your father was by my side and continued to be a wonderful father to you both.

Keep Fighting

We return to MD Anderson for a brain scan and a PET scan. I am a bit nervous, but not as much as last time. Tomorrow, I will find out the next step in my treatment. Regardless, I've made up my mind to accept it and continue to fight on like I have already done.

Today, I also learned of the death of a family member on my stepfather's side. I prayed for them and sent my mother a reading from a devotional with scripture. I cried because here I am fighting for life, and one life is gone. I'm still here, and God is still writing my story.

> I thought about these things. Then I understood that God has power over everyone, even those who are wise and live right.
>
> Anything can happen to any one of us, and so we never know if life will be good or bad. But exactly the same thing will finally happen to all of us, whether we live right and respect God or sin and don't respect God. Yes, the same thing will happen if we offer sacrifices to God or if we don't, if we keep our promises or are afraid to make them.
>
> It's terribly unfair for the same thing to happen to each of us. We are mean and foolish while we live, and then we die. As long as we are alive, we still have hope, just as a live dog is better off

than a dead lion. We know we will die, but the dead don't know a thing. Nothing good will happen to them-they are gone and forgotten. Their loves, their hates, and their jealous feelings have all disappeared with them. They will never again take part in anything that happens on this earth. So be happy and enjoy eating and drinking! God decided long ago that this is what you should do. Dress up, comb your hair, and look your best. Life is short, and you love your wife, so enjoy being with her. This is what you are supposed to do as you struggle through life on this earth. Work hard at whatever you do. You will soon go to the world of the dead, where no one works or thinks or reasons or even knows anything. Here is something else I have learned:

The fastest runners and the greatest heroes don't always win races and battles. Wisdom, intelligence, and skill don't always make you healthy, rich, or popular.

We each have our own share of misfortune. None of us know when we might fall victim to a sudden disaster and find ourselves like fish in a net or birds in a trap. (Ecclesiastes 9: 1–12 CEV)

Continue in Faith

On June 22, 2023, we woke up at 4:45 a.m. to make our appointment at 6 a.m. for the first scan of the day. I feel good and at peace during the scans. Later that day, the moment of truth came when I spoke with Dr. Valero.

He came in calmly with a document in his hand. He smiled and said, "Well, you already know the news of the brain MRI, and cells have disappeared. The PET scan shows no area in the body with cells, but in the sonogram, there is the small spot that is consistent and shows non-progression."

Dr. Valero says he is very happy with these results. I feel relieved and grateful to God for helping me through this difficult journey. Your father and I give each other a hug and thank God for all he has done.

My precious girls, all I could think about was how I longed to hear "free of cancer." Considering my stage, I have made tremendous progress by God's mercy and grace. When they told me the news of the scans, I was thankful beyond words. I prayed to God, telling him that I can never repay him and that I was ever so grateful. The past six months have been hills and valleys. Through those bad days, I held on, and it was only through God's grace and mercy. I'm so blessed!

Dear friends, God is good. So I beg you to offer your bodies to him as a living sacrifice, pure and pleasing. That's the most sensible way to serve God. Don't be like the people of this world, but let God change the way you think. Then you will know how to do everything that is good and pleasing to him.

I realize God has treated me with undeserved grace, and so I tell each of you not to think you are better than you really are. Use good sense and measure yourself by the amount of faith that God has given you. A body is made up of many parts, and each of them has its own use.

That's how it is with us. There are many of us, but we each are part of the body of Christ, as well as part of one another.

God has also given each of us different gifts to use. If we can prophesy, we should do it according to the amount of faith we have.

If we can serve others, we should serve. If we can teach, we should teach.

If we can encourage others, we should encourage them. If we can give, we should be generous. If we are leaders, we should do our best. If we are good to others, we should do it cheerfully. (Romans 12:1–8 CEV)

There is a song, "I'm So Blessed" by Cain, that we would sing and dance to. I used it as a daily reminder that God is in control and that there are many ways in which we are blessed.

You have never seen Jesus, and you don't see him now. But still you love him and have faith in him, and no words can tell how glad and happy you are to be saved. This is why you have faith. (1 Peter 1:8–9 CEV)

About the Author

Sarah lives in Deep South Texas. Feeling compelled to share her story, she took a leap of faith. She lives with her loving husband, two precious daughters, and two dogs, Max and Peaches. She enjoys reading, listening to music, and traveling.